Great! All the Time!

Gina,
go out there today and
be Great! All the time!

Great! All the Time!

Find peace and satisfaction
through the value-driven use of
life's precious resources

Kenneth R. Besser, J.D.

© 2007 Kenneth R. Besser, J.D. Printed and bound in the United States of America. All rights reserved. No part of this book may be reproduced or transmitted in any form or by any means, electronic or mechanical including photocopying, recording, or by an information storage and retrieval system – except by a reviewer who may quote brief passages in a review to be printed in a magazine, newspaper, television or radio program, or on the World Wide Web – without the publisher's written permission. For information, please contact RTMC Organization, LLC, Post Office Box 15105, Baltimore, Maryland 21282-5105, www.RTMC.org Telephone: 410-900-7834

Although the author and publisher have made every effort to ensure the accuracy and completeness of information contained in this book we assume no responsibility for errors, inaccuracies, omissions, or any inconsistency herein. Any slights of people, places or organizations are unintentional. This is a work of fiction, Any similarity to real people or events is purely coincidental.

Case bound - First printing 2007

ISBN 978-1-934316-01-6

LCCN 2006910611

ATTENTION CORPORATIONS, UNIVERSITIES, COLLEGES, AND PROFESSIONAL ORGANIZATIONS: Quantity discounts are available for bulk purchases of this book for educational or gift purchases or as premiums for increasing your effectiveness. Special books or book excerpts can also be created to fit your specific needs. For information, please contact RTMC Organization, LLC, Post Office Box 15105-5105, Baltimore, Maryland 21282, www.RTMC.org Telephone: 410-900-7834

Sol, the "King"

Anyone who greeted Sol more than a few times knew that, in response to their pleasant "How are you?", he was going to say to them, "Great! All the time!" Most were startled and surprised by the reply the first time they heard it. Some even wanted to argue with him about it by incredulously saying, "No you aren't. No one can be great all the time." This really puzzled Sol because he could never see what value they could possibly get out of trying to change his mind about it.

Many of those who greeted him often, by asking the perfunctory question, were more tired than not of the answer. Those who really knew him, however, and loved him despite it, knew that Sol truly was

Great! All the time!

No one really knew very much about Sol. Having reached the age at which society believes that

Great! All the Time!

most people should quit working a job everyday, Sol lived in the smallest one-room efficiency apartment available at the independent-living building on the community center campus.

Sol never talked about his past, what he had done for a living, or where his family was. All he did most days was walk around the building, volunteering for first one job or another at the center or the nursing home on the other side of the campus. Whenever anyone would ask him how he was on any given morning, afternoon, or night, Sol would just break out into a big smile and say, "I'm Great! All the time!"

Sol's biggest mission in his remaining years seemed to be to help lift everyone's spirits by giving them a smile. Sol would always make people smile back at him, whether they really wanted to or not. If someone wasn't smiling for whatever reason, Sol would go into his Mister Rogers mode. "Can you say 'Great!'?" he would ask, imitating the man's plain east coast accent, which everyone in America had come to know and love. "Sure you can."

Some people would really make Sol work hard to get a smile. If anyone said anything other than "Great!", then Sol would say, "Come on, try it. You know you can't really say 'Great!' without a smile."

If someone really had a reason not to smile, then Sol would sit with them talking quietly for as long as it took to understand what exactly was

Sol, the "King"

troubling them. Sometimes, it took a minute; sometimes, an hour. One time, the story is told around the nursing home, Sol sat with a lady for four hours letting her talk out all of the reasons why she felt like she was being warehoused in the home by her kids, who never called or brought her grandchildren to see her.

Eventually, however, everyone gave in and gave Sol the smile he wanted. Once he had gotten his smile, then Sol was off to conquer the next hill on his mission to make everyone he passed "Great! All the time!"

I first met Sol playing racquetball at the community center. Usually, every Sunday morning, after I finished getting a long, hard lesson in the game from someone or another, I would sit down on the bleachers opposite the racquetball courts and watch this reasonably fit old guy with a scraggly beard and balding head beat much younger players without even breaking a sweat.

Sol always gave the younger guy the first serve of the game. The younger guy would serve real hard and run around the court chasing every ball, while Sol just stood in the middle of the court, about ten feet from the back wall, and patiently waited for the ball to almost take its second bounce anywhere within five feet of him. Just as the ball was about to take its second bounce, Sol would stretch so far and bend so low that he would be able to catch the ball no more than one inch off the ground. He would

Great! All the Time!

smack it so hard to the front wall about two inches off the ground that it would almost always come out as a perfect rollout kill shot.

The younger guy would usually yell and cuss and bang his racquet against the floor or wall. Sol would just smile and serve one of his mixture of three serves, almost none of which ever came back out of the corner into which he put it. If the other guy did get his racquet on it and managed to return the serve, Sol didn't mind because he knew the ball would make itself available for a kill shot in the next volley or two. Some days, the younger guy would seem to be getting better. He would play more calmly and try to move Sol out of the middle of the backcourt. Sometimes, he would even score a few points.

One day, however, was different. Sol was playing a young kid who was as fast and accurate and low a player as he was. The kid played just like Sol, only from a position that was already much closer to the ground and much faster because he was so young. Sol gave him the first serve and the kid almost never came back out of the box in the middle of the court.

Almost all of his serves were perfect. Some would loop high off the front and side corner to drop over Sol's head and die in the back corner. Others would go like a rifle shot, ricochet low off the front wall, bounce once right behind the service line, and then do a rollout off the very bottom corner before

Sol, the "King"

the back wall. Others would work in a Z-shape off the front wall and die in the far back corner on the other side of the room. Apparently, this kid had been watching Sol for a long time, because he served and played just like old Sol did.

The kid was shellacking him, but Sol didn't seem to mind. It was almost like he was enjoying getting skunked. When the kid was done beating the old man, the two of them came out of the clear door in the glass wall.

The kid smiled at Sol and said, "Thanks, Mister Sol. Great game. I really enjoyed it."

"Me, too," Sol said, as he fell back into the bleachers next to me.

The kid then looked at me and asked, "How are you doing today?"

"Okay, I guess," I said, still soaked in sweat from my own game and looking plenty the worse for wear.

"Well, then you need to talk to this guy," the kid replied. "He can teach you how to go out there and be Great! All the time!" He smiled, as he headed off trotting down the hall.

I thought that I would gloat a little bit for the kid, because he wasn't doing it for himself, and pick on Sol for losing so badly to a punk.

"So, Mister Sol, how are you today, now that you just got beat by a kid a quarter your age and half your size?"

He looked at me and smiled. "Oh, me? I'm

Great! All the Time!

Great! All the time!"

"What do you mean you're great all the time?" I asked. "That kid just beat the heck out of you without even breaking a sweat."

"So?"

"So? So you're Sol, the King of the Court out here. You've been the league champion every year since you got here and you just got your jockstrap handed to you by a kid who can't be more than thirteen years old."

"He's twelve, actually," Sol said. "And I don't mind getting beaten by him because I helped him to learn the game."

"You taught him how to play like that?"

"Sure. Not only did I help him learn how to play racquetball like that, but also I helped him learn how to play life the same way. And not only did I help him learn how to play life, but through him I was able to help every other kid in his orphanage do the same thing as well. They were an absolute mess of a bunch of kids, but now they are just like me. They're Great! All the time!"

I was very skeptical about the whole thing. Nonetheless, if what he was saying was true, then you couldn't argue with the result that I just saw. I thought about it for a minute. My life was in a mess and I wasn't having much success over the long term at anything I was doing. So I figured I might as well try to see if maybe this guy could help me too.

"Can you teach me how to play like that?"

Sol, the "King"

"No."

"No?" I asked with a frown.

"No."

"Why not?"

"Because it's not something that can be taught," he said. "It's something you have to learn for yourself."

"Oh," I said. I was beginning to feel a letdown coming on.

"But, I can help you learn it for yourself, if you're willing to try."

"Good."

"It's not easy."

"That's okay. I've never been afraid of hard work. It's all I do all week."

"It's not a 'quick-fix' kind of a thing."

"That's okay, too. I've got lots of time. I'll just have to spend a little less time doing other things."

"You may have to give up a lot of stuff and change a lot of your attitudes about a lot of things."

"That's okay because, if you can teach me how to take a beating like that kid just gave you and like it as much as you did, then it must be worth doing

---

> Greatness! is not something
> that can be taught.
> You have to learn it for yourself.

7

Great! All the Time!

somehow."

"Okay."

"So, how do we get started?" I asked, wanting to begin immediately.

"We don't."

"We don't?"

"No, we don't." He started to get up. "You have to get yourself started first. First, you have to tell me the answer to 'What's your cha-ching?'"

"My what?" I asked.

"Your cha-ching."

"What's a cha-ching?" I asked again.

"Your cha-ching, man. What's your cha-ching; your value-based, visionary mission? Where do you want to go with this thing we call a life? Go home and write me a letter telling me what you want to do with your life."

"What do you mean 'What do I want to do with my life?'"

"Just that. Write me a letter telling me your values, vision, and mission. What you want to do

> You may have to give up a lot of stuff and change a lot of your attitudes about a lot of things.

8

Sol, the "King"

with your life? What is important to you? What do you want to accomplish in the few years that you are here on earth? How do you see yourself living a life according to your values? What exactly do you need to do in order to do so?" As he began to walk away to the locker room, he paused and added, "Think real hard for several days before you write it. Bring it back next week and we can play and talk."

I sat there for a minute or two, trying to figure out what it was he wanted me to do. I reviewed his questions in my mind. *What's my cha-ching, my value-based, visionary mission in life? What do I want to do with my life? What is important to me? What do I want to accomplish? How do I see myself living a life according to my values? What exactly do I need to do in order to do so?*

What's your cha-ching?

The First Letter

I went home and began thinking to myself. What is my cha-ching? What is my value-based, visionary mission in life? What do I want to do with my life? What is important to me? What do I want to accomplish? How do I see myself living a life according to my values? What exactly do I need to do in order to do so?

I had not really given much thought to these questions, which Sol had posed. I had pretty much just gone through life so far, doing whatever I could to get ahead in the circumstances that life presented me, without much of a plan about how to get there.

I had been to positive thinking, self-improvement, and similar seminars over the years, but they never seemed to work for me. It seemed that all of the other times, people were trying to tell me what I had to do in order to get ahead of everyone else; how to be a better executive, how to build a bigger business, and so forth.

Great! All the Time!

The speakers at the seminars usually said that you have to first think and decide something is important in order to achieve it, but no one had ever asked me, to really sit for a whole week and think about "What's my cha-ching?"

So I tried to do what Sol had asked me. I probed and pondered for quite a while. What is my value-based, visionary mission in life? What do I want to do with my life? What is important to me? What do I want to accomplish?

And so I thought for a few days while I went about the other tasks in my life. Get up. Go to work. Come home. Clean the house. Go to bed. Get up. Do it all over again. Go back to work. Work in order to have a place to sleep and food to eat. Eat and sleep to work some more. Try to build a better and bigger business to buy a bigger house, better cars, and more toys than the neighbors.

I thought about it all for the whole week. Saturday night, I sat down and started to write Sol his letter. I figured this was going to be one of the same exercises where I was supposed to write down what it was I wanted to do so Sol could give me the secret of how to accomplish it.

This is what I wrote.

The First Letter

Dear Sol,

I want to be a big success. I want to build a large company that either manufactures and/or distributes a consumable necessity. I want to employ lots of people providing these goods and services. I want to lead this army to greatness in the business world.

Obviously, I want to make a lot of money doing this because of the things it will let me buy for my company, my employees, my family, and myself. I would love to have a company plane in order to save time as I fly around the various locations of operations that I have, talking to my customers and my employees, encouraging them respectively to buy more and work harder.

It is important to me to be very well respected in my community. I want to be a "player" in business and politics. Having the respect of those in my neighborhood and my city is very important to me, because as Tevye says in Fiddler on the Roof, *"When you're rich, they think you really know." I want to be able to give money away so that others will ask my opinion about how best to run the government and charities in my community.*

I want to have the financial freedom to indulge my every whim and fancy. I want fine homes filled with fine art and furnishings. I want to own lots of land. I'd like to live life waking up as the king of my castle, having breakfast on the back deck of my home, and being able to look out on the horizon

Great! All the Time!

knowing that I own all that I survey.

But I don't want to have lots of things merely to have them. I want to use those things to motivate people. I went to an Amway meeting once. Those people sure know how to pump folks up and get them excited about selling soap. Anyway, I went to this meeting once and listened to this really rich guy who had been in the business for a long time.

The guy had just flown in for the meeting on his private jet and been brought from the airport in one of his associate's new Rolls Royce. They even drove him out onto the stage in the Rolls. When he got out of the car, the place exploded with everyone yelling his name over the loud music playing patriotic songs. He helped his wife out of the car and took off her mink coat and tossed it in the back seat. She sat down on the chair next to the podium while he started to quiet the people and let them hear him speak.

One of the things he said, which really impressed me the most, is "You can't love things instead of loving people." He said, "Things are not bad—it's the love of things that's bad. In fact, things are great as long as you use them to motivate people and help them be as successful as you are. Then everyone will own more things and be more successful and use all of their things to motivate others and so on."

I know I am going to have to work very hard to be the huge success I want to be in business. It will

The First Letter

take a lot of time away from my wife and my kids, but we don't get along too well anyway. Maybe they will love me more, if I can make a lot of money and give them whatever they want to make them happy.

So that's what I want to do with my life. That's my cha-ching. That's what's important to me and what I want to accomplish. I want to be a big success, buy lots of things and use them to help others be a big success with me, and buy my wife and kids whatever they want to make them happy.

The First Lesson

Sol was already warming up when I got to the court. I watched him practice his forehand serve, which had won him as many tournaments as all of his other moves on the court combined. Time after time, Sol hit a rifle shot, which would come off the front wall six inches up from the floor, bounce once right behind the service line, and then begin to roll toward the back.

After a while, he started doing something I had never seen anyone do before. I watched him go through the process of slowly getting ready to receive serves in the backcourt and then quickly lunge out to his forehand or backhand side and swing his racquet just like he was returning a maximally hit serve. Sometimes, he would move forward a few inches for the return. Other times, he would move back into a corner to catch a Z-serve. And still, other times he would go to the back wall to catch an imaginary lob serve falling from high to low.

Great! All the Time!

Sol noticed me standing there shaking my head in amazement. He stopped practicing and started to walk towards me through the clear door in the glass wall.

"How do you do that?" I asked, still shaking my head.

"Do what?"

"Make your serves die like that."

"It's just a matter of focus and balance," he explained. "Focus, and balance the right amount of placement, power, and backspin on the ball in each circumstance, and you will get the result you need."

"Okay," I said. "So what are all the imaginary service returns about?"

"What do you mean?"

"Well, most people practice returning Z-serves and lobs by hitting Z-shots and lob shots from the back and then returning them back to the front again."

"And, so?" Sol asked

"And, so you're not hitting anything. You're just jumping around the court."

"So?"

"So," I said. "You're not practicing hitting anything."

"I know."

"So what are you practicing?"

"Getting to it, now!" Sol said excitedly with a smile.

The First Lesson

"What?"

"Getting to it, now!" he repeated.

"What do you mean?"

"Do you remember how, sometimes, you know you should do something, but you tell yourself 'I'll get to it later'?"

"Yeah." I cracked a little bit of an embarrassed smile because I had thought, said, and done that more times than I cared to admit.

"Well, people who aren't 'Great!' keep trying to live in the future and they practice getting to it later, while people who are 'Great! All the time!' almost always live right here in the present and practice getting to it, now."

"Oh, I get it," I said. "But, you still aren't practicing hitting any real balls."

"No," he said. "But, what I am training myself to do, at the very second I am imagining a serve coming to me, is to think 'What is the highest and best use of my resources at this instant in time?' In the case of returning serves, the

---

> What is the highest and best use
> of your resources
> at this instant in time?

19

Great! All the Time!

highest and best use of my resources is to focus all of my self, time, effort, energy, emotion, intellect, property, and people available at that second on getting to the ball now. Not getting to the ball in a second and not how I am going to hit the ball when I do eventually get to it. The focus of my resources is just on 'Getting to it, now!' Do you see?"

"I think so," I answered, a little reticently.

"Anyone can turn a pretty good serve back into a volley, if they just get their racquet on it. The key is to get the racquet to the ball as soon as you know where it is going. When you have something to do, the main thing to think about is to 'Get to it, now!' The main thing I have to do to get a racquet on a well-hit serve is to 'Get to it, now!' It's not hitting the ball that counts. Anyone can hit a ball they get to. The main difference between my game and anyone else's game is I practice stretching myself to the absolute limit of my reach and I practice 'Getting to it, now!' Now, do you understand?"

"Yes," I replied, a little bit more surely.

Life's precious resources

Self, time, effort, energy, emotion, intellect, property, and people

---

The First Lesson

"It's the same way I live my life. I no longer wait to do in the future things I can do today. I live only for the present because I don't know when the Man upstairs is going to hit me with a Mack truck."

"But you can't get everything in life done today. You have to plan things for the future and get them done over a period of time."

"True," he agreed. "And you will ultimately succeed with that, but only so long as God doesn't get your attention with a bus and only so long as you get to doing today's steps in the planned process now. Not later today. Not tomorrow. Not later this week or someday. Get to it, now! Right now. Every time you start to do something you have to ask yourself 'Is this the highest and best use of my resources at this very moment to get my cha-ching?' If you can answer that question with an unequivocal 'Yes,' then you do it and if not, then you don't waste your resources."

"Can you teach me how to "Get to it,

Get to it, now!

Great! All the Time!

now!'?" I asked, wanting to get to the real lesson as soon as possible.

"Did you bring the letter?" he asked.

"Got it right here," I said, touching the outside pocket of my sports bag where it was sticking out.

"Good." He sat down, pulled it out, and started to open it. "I'll read it while you go warm up. Once I see that you have your values in order, a vision in line with those values, and a mission of concrete steps to make that vision a reality, then we can work on getting to it, now."

I went and practiced real serves, while Sol sat reading my letter. I could tell he wasn't enjoying it much because I kept looking back at him between serves and it looked like he just kept shaking his head back and forth as he finished each paragraph. He folded the letter, put it back in my bag, picked up his racquet, and came through the door to the court.

"So, how are you doing today?" he asked.

"I know you're going to keep on asking me unless I say I'm great, so I'm great so far today. Okay?"

"Great! But we'd better only make it a short game to eleven because I don't think you're going to be able to take much more than that our first time out. Okay?"

I nodded.

"You serve first," he said, as he planted himself in the middle of the backcourt. Then he

The First Lesson

added, "But you'd better make it a good one or it could be your last for the day because I'm already ready to 'Get to it, now!'"

I plowed a strong cross-court serve, which came out low to Sol's backhand and hit the sidewall just behind the service line. It looked like it was going to take a second bounce before it got to him in the middle of the backcourt. Still, Sol simply stretched as far as I had ever seen him stretch and smacked the ball with a backhand wrist shot, which went right back down the side wall, hit the front wall two inches above the floor, and began to roll out toward the service box.

Sol picked up the ball and began to bounce it getting ready to serve. "So you want to work real hard, have a big company with lots of employees, sell something to make a lot of money, and use it to make the world a better place. Is that about it?" He hit a serve that never came more than a foot off the ground.

"Yeah," I grunted, as I dove on my belly toward the side. I barely got my racquet on the ball before it was about to make its second bounce three-quarters of the way back down the forehand wall. I had no swing or power on the shot, but the speed of the serve and the angle of my racquet made the ball arch on a rebound almost all the way back to the front wall. Almost, but not quite enough.

"Good way to 'Get to it, now!'" he comforted me. "Just a little stronger next time."

Great! All the Time!

1-0 in favor of the old man.

Sol walked toward the ball, which had died in the front of the court. "Don't you think chasing money and things is just a little bit futile though?"

"No. Why?"

"Because, what good is it going to be to the world for you to put in all of that work just to own stuff?"

He hit another serve, this time to my backhand side, for which I was not ready. By the time I turned around from facing the front, the ball had already bounced twice and died in the back corner.

2-0 for the sage.

I picked up the ball and walked it back to him in the service box. "Because owning things is what motivates us to work hard." I put the orb in his hand. "I want to own my piece of this world. What's the use of making all of the money you do if you can't spend it on whatever you want? Besides, once I get the things, then I can use them to motivate others to work hard and get their own things too."

Sol stood up fairly straight and I knew a looping Z-serve was coming next. I moved to my backhand side to cut it off. He didn't look back to see where I was, so I thought I had this one for sure.

"And you think that is going to improve the world?" He dropped the ball from waist high. He must have heard me moving to get the Z-serve because he smacked a straight serve, which two-

The First Lesson

bounced on my forehand side before I could get over to it. He looked back at me still standing there in the backhand corner looking like a fool.

"Yeah," I said, walking to get him the ball, which had died in the back again.

3-0 for the senior partner.

As I walked it back to him again, he explained, "Well, pay attention and let me tell you this. What you are talking about is the futility of futilities."

"Why?" I gave him the ball and began to walk back to the middle of the backcourt.

"Because, what profit will you have for all of your work?" He bounced the ball a few times getting ready to serve. "You may think you are going to own your piece of the world, but it is still going to be here long after you are gone. You're no big shot in the scheme of things. People come and people go thinking they have owned their piece of the world, but it is still here after them. The sun will set without you. The wind will blow. The rivers will run. No matter how rich and successful you become, no one will know you have come and gone after you actually come and go."

Just as he was about to serve, I thought I would try to break his concentration. Sure, it wasn't sportsmanlike, but he was skunking me three-zip and he had just honked me off. "Tell that to Bill Gates and Warren Buffet!" I yelled.

The looping lob serve skimmed just an inch off the back of the wall and pinched back into it at

Great! All the Time!

the bottom as Sol watched me step backwards into the glass with a thud.

4-0 for the old man.

He smiled as I walked the ball back to him yet again. "Oh, really? Would you believe I used to be just as rich as you want to be and richer than they are or will ever be?"

"No."

"Well, I was. I was literally a king of my own castle. I was wise beyond all others and I indulged myself in every pleasure I wanted. I drank. I built businesses. I owned houses. I had thousands of employees. I had more money and things than even I could count. Everyone from all around looked up to me and asked me every question for which they ever needed an answer. And I thought I was as happy as I could be, doing everything I was doing."

I put the ball back into his hand. "And then?" I asked.

Sol turned to the forehand wall and telegraphed a low, fast forehand serve, which I was bound

---

> People come and people go
> thinking they have owned
> their piece of the world,
> but it is still here after them.

The First Lesson

and determined to catch. I started to dive low in anticipation, just to lay again on the floor and watch the ball loop over me along the wall and fall behind me. "And then, I looked at all the things I had done and the energy I had expended in doing them and it was clear; it was all futile and there is no real profit under the sun."

5-0 for the king of his castle.

I got up and started to walk the ball back to Sol again. "What do you mean there was no profit? You had it all, man. You had it made."

"Not really," Sol said. "What all did I have for my toil and stress in my work? All my days were painful, my business was a constant vexation, and all my nights were filled with the vexations of my days."

He took the ball and continued, "I would much rather have simply enjoyed whatever my work was and used my work to gain wisdom, knowledge, and joy than to foolishly chase a futile dream thinking I had to gather and amass as many possessions as I could."

I wondered what had happened to all of Sol's wealth. He lived in the retirement home instead of still living in the big house with all of the staff that I would have had if I were he.

"So what did you do with it all?" I asked, as he hit a forehand serve hard around himself and landed it behind me. I didn't much care about the ball because I was more interested in his story,

Great! All the Time!

which I had never heard before.

6-0 for the wise one.

"I chucked it, sold it, and closed it. Whatever it was, if it was material, then I got rid of it. And what was left, I handed down to my son; but, it being inherited wealth, he didn't really appreciate it and he blew it." The ball was rolling back to Sol. I wasn't moving much to get it, so he got it himself.

"Why did you chuck it?"

"Because I realized I was doing nothing but working only to have more and I wasn't working at something I enjoyed. Plus, I was so busy making a living, I had no time to make a life." He set up to serve again.

I moved a little toward the middle of the backcourt and nodded that I was ready for the next humiliation. It came quickly enough right at me. I moved to the side to avoid getting hit, but never had a chance at the return.

7-0 for the old man.

"So what did you do?"

Use your work to gain wisdom, knowledge, and joy.

The First Lesson

"I figured out there is nothing better than to be happy with one's lot and do good in life."

"And how do you do good in life."

"You eat and drink and find satisfaction in your work itself and not for the things it will bring you. Because you will never have satisfaction in things, but you will always have satisfaction if you are working on what's really important in life."

"And what is really important in life?"

"That which you would miss the most if you could never have it again."

"I don't understand."

"You will." Sol started to walk to the door. "That's 7-0. You've had enough for today. Go home. Really spend some time and think about what scares you the absolute most if you were to lose it and rewrite your letter about what's your cha-ching. What do you really want to do with your life, what is really important to you, and what do you really want to accomplish?"

I sighed with frustration at not having impressed him with my work so far and tried to follow him toward the locker room to talk some more. When I rounded the corner of the hall, however, Sol had already disappeared from sight.

The Second Letter

Nothing is more effective at making you focus and realize how truly important something is to you than facing the immediate and real possibility of losing that thing with absolutely no chance of ever being able to get it back again. I thought about this idea for a while and thought about everything I owned and how I would feel if I were faced with the immediate and real possibility of losing it.

I went through all of the calamities that could happen – someone stealing my car, breaking into my home or office to steal things, or burning down my house. Those were all material things, which I had insurance to replace. It would be inconvenient, but I could get them back. Then, I thought about some immaterial and irreplaceable things that could be lost – what if something happened to my wife or kids or even to myself?

It finally dawned on me; what is truly important in life is life itself and the relationships we have

Great! All the Time!

with the people, places, things, and ideas around us. If something happens to those around us or we let something permanently hurt our relationships, then we have truly lost something that cannot be replaced.

For many, unfortunately for most, such a situation usually involves the immediate and possible loss of their own life in the short or intermediate term due to a diagnosis of a heart attack, cancer, or some other dreadful disease. For others, the impending loss may be that of a loved one.

So far, I had only been forced to face such a loss twice in my life. Once was when the fourth of my six children fell fourteen feet from the second-story landing above the entry of our home to the marble floor below. Finding my six year-old lying on the cold slab, with blood running from the front and back of his head, instantly brought into focus what was truly important in life and, at that moment, it was the life of that child. I was sorry as I remembered it, however, because I had forgotten this lesson soon after I went back to work.

I had to face such a loss again when my wife was diagnosed with ovarian cancer. Though less emergent a circumstance, when faced with the fact that her ovaries, which were supposed to be the size of walnuts, had grown into masses the size of tennis balls, the fear of having to face the rest of my life without the other half of me was almost more than I could bear.

The Second Letter

Luckily, she had one of the least deadly types of ovarian cancer and she has now lived over a decade to tell the story. Nonetheless, there were many days of focused anxiety and anxious focusing during the weeks between the initial dreaded annual exam, the meeting with the surgeon where we reviewed whether he thought he had "gotten it all," and the later follow-up discussion of the pathology report, which only gave us a one-in-six chance of having this particular cancer reoccur. (Anyone for a daily game of Russian roulette?)

During that time, my wife and I sought solace in and received great healing from almost every relationship we had going at the time. Those relationships included our God, each other, our children, parents, family, true friends, community, employees, customers, and someone else that I had not really talked to seriously for a good long time – myself.

While talking to myself and to the others who were supporting us, I realized my wife and I had strayed from some of the principles we had espoused more stridently in the past. Many of the things we were doing at the time no longer made much sense. The things such as an expensive home, cars, fine furnishings, and clothes, upon the accumulation of which we had increasingly become focused, gave us absolutely no comfort in our time of need.

It was the large number of people and the extensive relationships we had enjoyed with them

Great! All the Time!

over the years that were sustaining and supporting us. The people around us, through acts and deeds both small and large, were helping to hold our lives together in ways we had never imagined. They were giving us significant amounts of their own precious resources of self, time, effort, energy, emotion, intellect, property, and people. All of the people around us were simply wonderful and their helping us through that time was more valuable than we could ever repay.

Some time after the anxiety subsided, I began to reflect on what had happened, how our circle of great people had responded and how we could ever repay them. But I never did. I just went back to work, chasing more dreams of having more things. Working harder to build bigger kingdoms to rule.

And then it dawned on me that Sol was exactly right. If I was going to find peace and satisfaction in life, then I was going to have to change my thinking and not work to have more things. I was going to have to change and find some way to work for the

> It is our relationships that sustain and support us.

The Second Letter

sake of being satisfied with my work itself.

And so I wrote.

Dear Sol,

I got it! I sat down and started to think about the things in my life that scared me the most when I almost lost them and, guess what? They were all relationships - relationships with myself and everyone around me.

I thought about the time my wife almost died and how much it scared me that I might have to be alone in life without her. But then I realized I would not be totally alone because there were relationships all around me, which I had taken for granted; relationships with God, with my wife, with our children, with our parents, with our family, with our true friends, with our community, with our employees, with our customers, and even with myself.

But I think I may have already lost some of those relationships by working all the time. I have been working for the wrong reasons. You've shown me that all labor and all skillful enterprise spring from my rivalry with my neighbors – to have more than they do. This is, as you said, futile. It's not having more than the Joneses that counts. It's having enjoyable work to do and having someone enjoyable with whom to do it.

Relationships, Sol. They are what is important. Two people working together get a greater return

Great! All the Time!

for their labor, if they are concertedly trying to make the world a better place instead of trying to get a leg up on each other.

Relationships, Sol. Building relationships is what I want to do with my life. Relationships are important to me. Having good relationships is what I want to accomplish.

So, Sol, now I know. I want to have great relationships, but I still have to work in order to eat, drink, and enjoy those relationships.

Tell me, how do I go about doing that?

The Second Letter

> What are you
> most afraid to lose?

The Second Lesson

Sol was ahead of me again the next Sunday. I didn't wait for him to come off the court to let me warm up. I just tapped on the glass door and started to walk in. As I entered, he stopped in mid-serve and stood up to look at me.

"How are you today?" he asked.

"Great!" I answered. I was pumped and ready to go.

"Did you bring your new letter?"

"Yes, I brought the letter, but you don't need to read it." I walked toward the server's box. "Give me the ball, man. Let's play this game!"

Sol smiled and said, "Well, alright!" as he put the ball in my hand.

I squeezed the blue rubber rascal so I could feel how much power was in it. I let it drop toward the floor and said, "Relationships, Sol," as I smacked a rifle shot low to his backhand side.

"What?" he asked, as he very quickly but

Great! All the Time!

seemingly effortlessly stretched over to slap the shot back high to the front.

"Relationships," I repeated, as I ran all the way to the back to get the ball and keep the volley going. "You told me to think about what I most feared losing and it's something I think I may have somewhat already lost."

I hit the ball hard but straight back along the same wall, trying to keep it all the way over and draw Sol out of his spot; but he just stretched out to it after only moving one foot. "And that is?"

"It's losing my relationships with everyone around me that scares me the most." I went back to my forehand again. "I have to use all of my ..." I closed in for the kill. "Power!..." I smacked the heck out of it. "To work on my relationships with everyone around me."

Too much power can also be a bad thing, I thought to myself as the ball hit the front wall, the side wall, and the back wall in quick succession, and then fell dead in the middle of the court. Sol picked it up and moved to the server's box.

I thought to myself, "I'm still ahead zero to zero."

"Well, you've got the power down enough for today," Sol said, letting the ball drop and sending his own rifle shot past my backhand faster than I could catch it. "Let's see if we can work on the control."

I picked the ball up and walked it back to Sol, with the air letting out of my Jordans.

The Second Lesson

1-0 for the controller.

"Okay," I said, putting the ball back in his hand. "How can I learn about control?"

"You can't yet."

"Why not?"

"Because, before you learn about control, which is actually just a matter of balance, you have to learn about targeting."

"Targeting? What do you mean?"

"I mean you have to think about targeting before you can do anything," he said. "How can you hit anything if you don't first figure out what you are aiming for?"

I looked around the ceiling of the front half of the court for a second and then looked back at Sol. "So what should I be aiming for?"

"Well, whatever you do, you want to be doing the right thing."

Sol let loose a funky Z-serve, which almost hit me in the head as I backed up to catch it in the far backhand corner. I sent it high and back down the same wall to make the old guy come and get it before it came back out from the back wall. Sol turned around and caught the ball coming off the glass and hit it back to rollout from the front.

2-0 for the solon.

Sol stayed facing me as the ball rolled past him and back towards me.

I asked, "Okay, so what is the right thing?" I bent over to pick up the ball and walked it back to

Great! All the Time!

him.

"The right thing," Sol said, holding the ball in his palm with his thumb and pointing with the rest of his fingers for emphasis, "is doing whatever is best in the present circumstances for the optimal balance of the highest and the most of those to whom …" He pointed up with his index finger and then lowered his hand and moved it like he was smoothing troubled waters in front of him. "And for whom our values make us responsible."

Sol turned and bent over as he started to get ready to serve. As I started to back up to the middle of the backcourt, I stopped him. "What?" I asked a little bit loudly.

He stood back up. "Do you want me to go back over that again?"

"Yes, please." I took a half step closer to hear him.

"The right thing," he repeated, still holding the ball with his thumb in his palm, "is doing whatever is best in the present circumstances for the

---

The right thing

is doing whatever is best in the present circumstances for the optimal balance of the highest and the most of those to whom and for whom our values make us responsible.

The Second Lesson

optimal balance of the highest and the most of those to whom … ," index finger up, "and for whom … ," fingers smoothing the waters, "our values make us responsible."

"Okay," I nodded tentatively while stepping back.

Sol served the ball low down the forehand wall. I stretched as far as I could, first, with my leg and ,then, with my shoulders and my racquet. I just caught it at the farthest reach of my swing to send it back down the wall for the first really good rollout service return I had hit in a long time.

I picked up the ball and began walking it back to take my place in the service box for a change. "And who are those to whom and for whom our values make us responsible?" I pointed up and then calmed the waters with a respectful smile on my face as I turned back to serve.

Just as I was about to let go of the ball, Sol said, "All of those whom you just discovered are most important to you."

I felt some power coming to me in my swing. I let loose a rocket serve, which shwooshed by, right off the wall, as it zipped past his fully stretched backhand. It happened so fast that I didn't really have much time to enjoy it. I looked back and saw Sol, still all stretched out, with his racquet just a hair more than a ball's width from the wall, looking at the ball die off in the back corner and roll back to him. He smiled a knowing smile as he took the ball,

Great! All the Time!

stood up, and walked it back to me in the service box.

1-1. Back even with the old guy.

He handed me the ball and I asked, "So all of those with whom we have relationships are the ones to whom and for whom our values make us responsible?" I made a quick point of one finger up followed by a nippy one-fingered smoothing of the waters.

"Exactly," he answered, setting himself up for my next serve. "To some degree."

I set up looking like I was going to go strong to his forehand. "But how do I know who is the highest in order to figure out the 'highest priority and the most' part?"

I let the ball drop, then changed up in the middle of the swing and wrapped a serve back around myself to the same spot on the backhand wall.

Sol missed the return again. I tried not to smile while I looked back to see him. He was trying to get just two more inches of stretch out of his stance, which was almost a split as it was.

1-2 in favor of the middle-aged student.

He flipped the ball back to me. "Well, take a look at your relationships and see which are dependent on the others."

"What do you mean?"

I figured he would think I wouldn't try the same spot three times, so I did it anyway to try and

The Second Lesson

fool him. The result was less than good. He got all the way over to it, ripped it back down my backhand for a rollout, and took his first step back toward the service box all in one knowing motion.

"Who are your relationships with?" he asked, as he waited for me to go chase the ball.

"God, my wife, my kids, my parents ... ," I began, as I played retriever and handed him the ball. "My family, some true friends, my community ... " I stepped back to receive the serve. "My employees, my customers, and myself." I finished just as Sol's next serve flashed past me like a bullet.

2-2 dead even, again.

"And who is dependent on whom?" he asked, holding out his hand for the ball in the corner.

"I don't understand what you're asking," I said, getting the ball.

"Well, let's handle the easy one first. Would God exist without a relationship with you or any of the other relationships you listed?"

I put the ball in his hand. "Yes."

"So then He is the highest thing there is, right?"

"Right," I agreed, as I heard the next serve, but didn't really see it go by. All I saw was the ball rolling in the back of the court. I flipped it back to him.

3-2 in favor of the scraggly-bearded wonder.

"Would any of your relationships exist without you?"

Great! All the Time!

"No." I heard the next serve and saw it go by, but still wasn't fast enough to get it.

4-2 in favor of the professor.

"So, you must be next in the list of your priorities after God, right?" Sol turned to serve again.

"I guess so, but that seems contrary to what I've always been taught about putting others first."

"You can't take care of anyone else ... ," Sol started to say, as he plinked a Z-serve just long enough to crash me into the back wall. "If you don't take care of yourself, first." I moved to get the ball for him. "But, that's part of balance and we're still on targeting your priorities."

I mimicked under my breath, "That's part of balance and we're still on targeting."

5-2 in favor of the crotchety one.

"But, what about my wife, my kids, and my parents?" I asked, as I took the ball back to him again. "They all seem to be on the same level to me?"

"Not really." Sol floated a high serve to me and I finally got a volley started. "Could you marry your wife without your parents?" he asked.

"Yes."

"Then she's independent of your parents." Sol held the middle ground and kept the volley going by running me around. "Could you have the kids you have now without your wife?"

"No," I panted, from the back of the court.

The Second Lesson

"Who do you expect to leave your closeness first – your wife, your kids, or your parents?" He held the center still.

I missed the next shot and stopped to catch my breath. "I expect my parents to leave first because I left them to marry my wife. I expect my kids to leave next because they will leave our house when they grow up."

6-2 in favor of the king.

Sol motioned for the ball. "So, based on the closeness to you and the expected proximity and longevity of the relationship, it looks like the priority is wife, kids, parents, right?"

I put the ball in his hand. "I guess the rest of my family comes next?"

"Unless they are so far removed in closeness that a true friend makes up for it in proximity and longevity." Sol zipped another one past me leaving me flat footed.

7-2 in favor of the elder.

"And I guess my community, my employees and my customers come next?" I trotted off for the ball and back again.

"Same thing. What do you want to last the longest? Is your business more important than the community in which you live? No. Who would you rather keep the longest? Employees or customers?" Sol tried to sneak one past my backhand again, but I kept it in play.

"Customers," I answered, as I made the shot.

47

Great! All the Time!

"The customer is always right and I can always get more employees."

"Wrong!" Sol replied loudly, as he slapped another rollout into the front wall. "Can your customers help you get and keep good employees?"

8-2 in favor of the leader.

"No." I retrieved another ball.

"Exactly. Good employees are higher because they can help you get and keep loyal customers, but customers are very fickle and will always leave in the end for a cheaper price or a newer, better product."

Sol finally served one I could hit.

I made the return into a kill shot and got into the service box again. I was feeling very powerful with what I had just learned and began zipping a few more serves past Sol. Before long, I had evened the score to 8-8 and then we bounced back and forth until he was serving to me for the game point.

As he was about to serve, I asked, "But, how do I know when to be doing what? When do I work on my relationships with my wife and kids and when do I work on my business and my relationships with my employees and customers?"

I lobbed a return over his head and watched him move to the center of the backcourt like he always does. I thought I had him beat because the pinch shot in the front ceiling hit the floor way up front and was lobbing far over Sol's head.

"That, my friend," Sol started to say, as he jumped up higher than I had ever seen someone of

The Second Lesson

his age and stature jump before. He dinked the kill shot and then landed, balanced on the end of the toe of his left shoe, with the racquet in his right hand still held as high as possible. "Takes balance." He held the pose for more than a few seconds to make sure I had appreciated what he had just done. "Which is something we will discuss next week after we talk about the relationships between life's precious resources."

I scrunched up my brow and asked, "What precious resources?"

"Your own personal resources of self, time, effort, energy, emotion, intellect, property, and people."

"Why not talk about that now?"

Sol checked his watch. "Because you haven't thought about it yet and I have to go help serve lunch to us old folks." He walked out the door, stopped, looked back at me, and pointed. "Go back home and, this week, write me another letter about how you use your self, time, effort, energy, emotion, intellect, property, and people to do the best thing for the optimal balance of the highest and most of those to whom and for whom your values make you responsible."

He started to walk down the hall and leaned his head back to yell at the ceiling and me, "And, while you're at it, go out there this week and be Great! All the time!"

The Third Letter

I thought about the relationships I had discussed with Sol for the rest of the day. As the week progressed, I found myself working a lot less and doing a lot more of other things with those who had higher priority relationships with me.

On Monday, I told my employees to make sure they left and went home to their own families on time from then on. Then, I went home for dinner. On Tuesday, I decided to start going in to work at a normal eight o'clock instead of six so I could go to prayers each morning. On Wednesday, I took off early in the mid-afternoon and went to my kids' basketball games at school. On Thursday, we all went to some friends' house for an early dinner and then we all volunteered filling orders at the food bank for most of the night.

My days of work, work, work, seemed to be subsiding, but, by Friday, my company's sales were down for the week and I started to have

Great! All the Time!

second thoughts about all of this highest and most responsibility stuff.

For the entire week, I thought to myself, how should I use all of my resources of self, time, effort, energy, emotion, intellect, property, and people to do the best thing for the optimal balance of the highest and the most of those to whom and for whom I was responsible?

I was hoping that maybe some intense thought about the question Sol had posed would give me some comfort. So, I left the office Friday at noon to go to the park and sit and think and write.

Dear Sol,

You told me to think about and answer your question, which is essentially "How should I use all of my life's precious resources to do the right thing?"

I've thought a long time about the question and I realize now that I have to balance and prioritize the relationships in my life and then balance and prioritize the use of my resources in order to best serve the needs of those to whom and for whom I am responsible.

The more I think about it, however, the more it seems like spinning eight plates while juggling thirteen snakes. How do I balance and prioritize the use of my self, time, effort, energy, emotion, intellect, property, and people to do what is the best thing for the optimal balance of the highest and the most

The Third Letter

of my God, self, spouse, children, parents, family, true friends, community, investors, employers, employees, customers, and a mission driven by a vision based on values?

Frankly, Sol, I have no idea how to go about doing it. At least I feel comfortable enough with you to tell you this. I hope you can help me put things in some kind of order.

The Third Lesson

    I strolled up to the bleachers outside the racquetball courts with a little less punch than I had the week before. Sol was continuously hitting the same ball in lots of different directions for many shots, all of which kept returning right back to him. As he turned around to place one against the back wall, he noticed me, caught the ball coming back at him with his free hand, and pocketed it as he came out to greet me.

    "How are you today?" he asked.

    I only hesitated for a fraction of a second before replying with just the tiniest of a sigh. "Great! All the time!" I answered him. I then added, "But some days it's much more difficult than others to say that."

    "I know," he said, with a knowing smile. "There's a lot more to it than you thought there'd be, isn't it?"

    "How'd you know?"

Great! All the Time!

"A lot of people get stuck at this point and just give up."

"I'm not giving up!" I objected, feeling guilty now about wimping out in my letter.

Sol smiled at me again, as he held out his palm. "So let's see what you wrote," he demanded.

I pulled the letter out of my bag's pocket and gave it to him. "It basically says that I have no idea what we are talking about and I need a lot of help."

He chuckled and grinned, as he unfolded the single sheet of paper. "Then you're just like I was when I was your age." He read it quickly and then said, "Thanks for the compliment about feeling comfortable enough to ask."

"So what's it all about, Mister Sol? Help me understand it."

"Okay," he said. "Do you need a warm up?"

"Today, I think I do."

"All right, we'll just knock it around the court a little bit first. But whatever you do, don't let the ball stop. Okay?"

Sol stood three-quarters of the way back in the court and sent a soft easy shot to me on my forehand side. "So what do you know about your life's precious resources?"

"The way I see it," I started to explain, as I eased the ball to the front wall and back to him, "is we all basically have the same types of resources you listed; self, time, effort, energy, emotion, intellect, property, and people." We traded volleys

The Third Lesson

between thoughts as I continued. "We all have a self, which we can motivate to act. We all have the same amount of time in a day, week, month, or year. We all can make an effort to use our energy to do work. If we use our emotion and intellect effectively, then we can use our self, time, effort and energy to create property, including money and things. The only other category of resource that you spoke of is people, who technically we can attract or create and grow using self, time, effort, energy, emotion, intellect, other property, and other people."

Sol shifted from hitting the front wall to attacking the front of the ceiling so we could chase lobs for a while. "So what's your problem then?"

I reached over my head and pointed to follow the ball and let a soft, long stroke take it back to the teacher. "The questions that bother me most, however, are how do I decide how much of what resources to use when and which of two competing responsibilities should be satisfied?"

Sol didn't say anything except for "Uhm-hmm," as he sent the ball up into the front ceiling and back to me.

"What I mean," I went on, as we passed the shot back and forth, "is how much of each kind of resource should I invest in each of my major ongoing projects; such as, being better at my religion, being a better husband, father, son, friend, or citizen, or having a better business with better employees and customers? All of those relationships seem to need

Great! All the Time!

constant care and feeding, and I am only one man with a limited amount of those resources."

Sol changed directions a little and began sending me three-wall shots. "So, what's your problem then?" he asked again.

"Like most others …" I kept on talking, as I sent the new shots back. "I have a house and cars to pay for; a family, which needs to be fed and clothed and wants to be bought the niceties of life; and a business, which I have to stay at and watch all the time. Until this week, I've only had time to pray once a week on Sabbath. Each of the things I want to do in life and any one of my relationships could individually take up all of my time if I let it. So, I guess I'm going to have to learn how to prioritize my relationships, first, and then figure out how to balance the use of my resources to move all of my projects along and take care of all of my relationships, a little at a time, but, still, all the time. That's the trick of the thing. That's what's stumping me." I stopped for a long inhale.

"Well, welcome to the club," Sol finally responded, without telling me a thing.

"What club?"

"The club of life after the garden?"

"What garden?" I asked, as I sent the ball back down my backhand side, making Sol move over behind me to get to it.

He sent a crosscourt shot the opposite way I had, moving me to the other side of the floor. "The

The Third Lesson

Garden of Eden, son," he informed me. "It's just not as easy as it was originally planned."

I sent a shot back down the middle and pleaded, "So help me out here a little bit."

Sol glanced at me for a split second, as he turned around, hit the ball going past him off the back wall, and urged it to speed up and arch well toward the front of the court. As he did, he said, "First, let's review what we said about your relationships, to see which are the highest and the most of those to whom and for whom you are responsible."

"Okay," I agreed, as I chased toward the front and put the ball back toward him again.

As he hit another rear wall shot, Sol continued, "Each of us is responsible to our self and at least some of those around us. Correct?"

"Correct," I replied, feeding him again.

We passed the ball back and forth off the rear and front walls as I nodded at each of his statements.

"In addition to our self and the people around us, to whom and for whom our values make us responsible, there are some intangible things, such as ideas, values, or beliefs, to which and for which our values make us responsible. True?"

"True," I nodded. "But we did all of this last week.

Sol continued to push balls interspersed with ideas at me. "The natures, types, quantities, and priorities of those responsibilities may ebb and flow

Great! All the Time!

and otherwise change, from time to time, depending on our circumstances. Right?"

"Right."

"We may or may not have a religious grounding. We may or may not be married. We may or may not have living parents or children. We may or may not have investors, employers, employees, or customers. We may or may not have a core value system."

I hit a soft shot and then ran back toward the back wall to steal it back for myself. "We all have a core value system," I corrected him, as I helped my own rebound become a new shot to him, back where I left him in the front. "Some of them are just not as good as others."

"Nonetheless," he replied, moving to where I sent him, "the average Joe or Josephine out there is at least a minimally religious, married person, with one or two children, at least one living parent, and a few true friends."

"Yeah," I responded, going along, as I sent him some more balls as well.

"He lives in a community. She has a job at a company with investors, one or more bosses above her, one or more employees underneath her, and customers. He has some set of core values that says some intangible things have significance and are worth spending resources on. She has some vision of how to live a life in accordance with those values. He has some mission consisting of steps required to

The Third Lesson

fulfill that vision."

"Okay," I agreed, hitting another back-wall shot, trying to land it lower on the front wall.

Sol turned back toward the front and we went back to easy forehands again.

"Given such a scenario," he said, "we learned last week that the average Joe or Josephine's responsibilities and priorities may be listed as follows: God, self, spouse, children, parents, family, true friends, community, investors, employers, employees, customers, and a mission driven by a value-based vision."

"Yes, we did," I said, squatting down to hit lower shots. "But what are the essences of those things and how do I balance between them?"

Sol caught the ball going by with his free hand and then looked at me while feigning exasperation. "So now you want to talk about the essence of life?" he asked me, with a small grin.

"Just to make sure that we're both on the same page."

> The average Joe or Josephine's responsibilities and priorities may be listed as follows:
> God, self, spouse, children, parents, family, true friends, community, investors, employers, employees, customers, and a mission driven by a value-based vision.

Great! All the Time!

"Are you sure you want to get off into that this week? You look kind of tired," he said, nodding toward my sweat-darkened shirt.

I accepted the unspoken challenge. "I can last as long as you can," I boldly assured him.

"Yeah, right," he said, with a knowing broad smile. He sent a pinch shot up to the top right corner, which then jammed back down on me.

I was only quick enough to get my racquet on the ball and it ended back up in Sol's lap. He sent it back into the same ceiling corner and said, "All right, let's start with God."

I hit the ball fast and hard enough into the center of the front ceiling to bounce it off the floor and over Sol's head. As he moved back to his usual parking place in the center back court, I asked him, "You're not going to try and convert me, are you?"

"Nah," he said, slapping a rollout kill shot back past me. "I'll let you try and convert me." He walked over, picked up the ball coming to him, and stepped up into the service box. "But enough of this warm-up stuff. Let's play for some points."

I shook my head a little, as I walked back to receive a serve. "Okay, but it's hard to talk about this and play for points at the same time."

"That's okay," he said. "Relax, and I'll pause between points so you can talk."

Sol plastered a serve along my backhand wall, which I was just able to nail right back down the same line to take him out.

The Third Lesson

"You relax," I said, scooping up the ball with my racquet while I smirked. "I'll pause between points."

"So what do you know about God?" he asked, moving back past me to his favorite spot.

I bounced the ball a few times. "I don't know," I said, as I served a Z to Sol's backhand. "All of us need to believe in something bigger than ourselves."

"Why?" He asked sending the ball hard into the back wall and up to the bottom of the front wall again. "Why believe in Him?"

I ran and dove to catch the ball with my racquet, before its second petering bounce; but all I accomplished was to place the return straight down the middle, where Sol killed it for a rollout.

"Why?" I repeated his question to him. "I don't know. Because six hundred thousand Jews in the desert over three thousand years ago, could not have been misled?"

"Ah, so does believing in God only apply to the Jews?"

"No," I said defensively, having answered this question many times before. "God knows no sectarian boundaries. While my personal religious perspective is as a committed Jew, the concept of a higher being is compatible with any religion or belief. In the traditional Jewish, Christian, and Muslim scheme of things, God is the universal deity, from which flows absolutely everything in the world

Great! All the Time!

according to God's will, regardless of whether we truly understand the reason for it or not."

"And, what about those who don't believe in God?" Sol asked, as he creamed an ace past me.

It whizzed by so fast that I was only able to move my racquet halfway toward its line before it went on and died in the corner.

"You have to 'Get to it, now!" he advised.

As I walked slowly toward the ball, I answered, "For those who profess to have no deity or religion manifest in their life, they can insert whatever higher power, collective unconsciousness, or philosophical explanation for how and why things happen in the world, as the ultimate non-corporeal entity, to which our values make us responsible." I then slowly walked the ball back to Sol. "Regardless of what they consider it to be, something set this miraculous world in order and manages, despite our constant conscious or unconscious attempts to destroy it, to keep it running and all of us living in it. For the sake of having an easy common reference, however, let us continue to refer to the ultimate non-corporeal entity as God. Okay?"

"Okay," he agreed, as I dropped the ball into his hand. "So how does God play into our lives?"

Sol looked back at me to see if I was ready to receive his serve. I nodded and beckoned him to bring it to me with my racquet. He set up for my backhand side and then slapped a change-up to my forehand. As soon as I saw his hips shift direction, I

The Third Lesson

didn't even pay attention to the ball. I just dropped down into a near split to my forehand side, stretched my racquet all the way to the wall, cocked it back, and hammered the ball back to the front forehand corner for a rollout of my own.

As I scooped up the quickly rolling ball with my racquet, I turned back to Sol from the service box and answered, "From studying and attempting to know more about God, we are able to draw our sense of self and self worth, our sense of right and wrong, and our sense of peace with the order of life that goes on around us."

I bounced the ball a few times and then zipped a serve as straight and as fast as a bullet down Sol's backhand wall. He brought the ball back to me with a look that said he had enjoyed all he wanted to in the backcourt.

I finished my explanation. "As we come to understand more about what it is that God expects of us, in return for His precious gift of our part in this world and the world to come, we must realize that our values make us responsible to God, to maximize ourselves, to do what we perceive to be the right thing, based upon that knowledge."

"All very circuitous," he retorted, "but we'll let that go for now." Sol put the ball in my hand, as he asked, "What about your concept of self?"

"What about it?" I inquired, as I served a high one, which bounced off the front wall and the ceiling, then behind the service line, and, finally,

Great! All the Time!

over Sol's head.

Sol rested his racquet flat against the back wall and whipped it forward, just as the ball passed in front of it. "What about it?" he parroted my question back to me, as the ball died in a pinch in the front forehand corner. "Satisfaction with your life can only be achieved for yourself," he explained, as he walked toward the dead ball. "And in order to achieve satisfaction for yourself, you must put responsibility to yourself immediately below your responsibility to God, and ahead of all others."

"Isn't that being quite selfish?" I asked.

"No," he replied. "It's called practicing personal primacy."

"Does that mean you should always put yourself first and ignore your responsibility to others?" I asked, as he went by.

"No, it means you have to plan on taking care of yourself, first, so you can then take care of others. Also, it means, if something you are asked to do for others may permanently hurt you, then you

---

Satisfaction with your life can only be achieved for yourself.

The Third Lesson

should be absolutely sure the reason you are doing it and the benefits from doing it are worth the costs and risks of doing it."

Sol picked up the ball and took a giant step back into the service box. He paused momentarily and asked, "So, what did we say came next after God and yourself?"

"Your spouse."

"And, so?"

"And, so what?" I posed.

"So, tell me about your spouse?" he said, as he sent a high serve over my head along my backhand wall.

I moved back, waited for the ball to return off the back wall between bounces, and then shot it right back up into the front ceiling from whence it came.

"A movie released some years ago, called *The Butcher's Wife*," I started to say, as Sol moved over and made the same shot I just had, "told a story of a man and a woman who were just meeting."

You must practice
personal primacy.

Great! All the Time!

Sol came back and made the same shot again, so I just stayed nearby and practiced my backhand ceiling return while I continued. "The woman told the man she was looking for her 'split-apart,' which she explained was the other half of her soul, which God had split apart from hers and put in a man. Her mission in life was to find her split-apart, fall in love with him, and marry him."

Sol slid back in behind me and then killed the shot to the other side of the court. As he walked back up to the ball again, he asked, "So you think your wife is your 'split-apart'?"

I nodded with a quizzical grimace. "Hokily romantic as it may sound, yes," I answered, as he moved back to set up his next slaughtering serve and waited for me to finish. "I was lucky to have found my 'split-apart' at the early age of seventeen. I knew she was the one for me as soon as I met her. She took a little longer to come around to the idea, though." I grinned sheepishly. "Nonetheless, she is the second most important person in the world to me. My wife has loved me and supported me pretty much unconditionally for thirty years and everything I am and everything I am able to do is due in large part to her love and support. She was with me before we had children and she will be with me long after both our parents and our children have gone their respective ways. Therefore, after God and myself, my spouse is the next highest relationship I have."

"Right answer," Sol said. As he cut a sidespin

The Third Lesson

serve at me, he added, "And for ten bucks, I'll tell her you said so."

I had never seen a serve make a ninety-degree turn as it hit the floor. I just stood there, motionless, as I watched it change direction toward the sidewall between Sol and me, and then bounce back to the center court.

"How did you—?" I started to ask looking at the ball just merrily bouncing inches off the floor toward Sol.

"Just focus, balance, power, and spin control," he said, grinning as he used his racquet to make the ball dance in several directions and bounce right back to him. "It's the secret to appropriately using your resources." He finished with one slice of his racquet, which sent the ball to both sidewalls in turn. "I taught the same thing to Chi Chi Rodriguez in the sixties," he grinned. He bounced the ball a few more times up and down on the floor with his hand. "So, as we were saying, your order is God, yourself, your spouse, then what?" He lofted another soft serve to my forehand side and we began another rally.

"Then children, parents, and the rest of the family, for all of the same reasons."

"Such as?" Sol asked, as he extended the volley with another creampuff pass, which I slapped along to the back wall.

"Well, almost anyone can be a father or a mother, but it's much more difficult to be a 'mom' or a 'dad'. When you decide to be a mom or dad to your

Great! All the Time!

children, then you agree to be totally responsible for them for your entire life. For real parents, as opposed to mere 'biosources,' their children are their highest priorities right after their spouses."

"Fine, then," Sol said, banging his own shot to the back wall. "And parents?"

"Same thing, only in reverse," I said, taking off for the front of the court to catch his shot, which was about to brush the front wall and die. I pinched the ball off the front backhand corner to end the side again. "If we have living parents, and they were and are good parents, then they have been and continue to be the source of much of our resources in this world, and are deserving of our love, respect, and help, in return for what they have given us. So we need to be sure that we don't take our parents for granted and forget our responsibilities to them."

"Why not?" Sol requested.

I picked up the ball and walked back to the service box to get ready again. "If we are blessed with both children and living parents, we have a vested interest in being sure our kids see us taking especially good care of our folks, as they grow older and become more needy of care."

"Why?"

"Because, it will happen much too soon that our parents become our children and we, in turn, will become our children's children. Hence, we have some self-interest in making sure that our kids know how to take care of this particular responsibility."

The Third Lesson

Sol smiled broadly, like I had just said something either especially smart or more especially stupid. I smiled back as I tried a sidespin serve of my own. The ball misbehaved and landed to take its turn much too far before the service line.

"Short," Sol said, as he scooped the ball back to me. "Focus, balance, power and spin control," he instructed. Then he added, "Try again."

I tried the same serve a second time. It landed a little bit closer to the service line, but not close enough. "Side out," Sol said, scooping up the ball again. "Focus, balance, power, spin control, and practice, practice, practice."

"Now," Sol started to say, as he began to wind up a serve and then stopped before ending his backswing. "What about the rest of your family and friends?"

"Same thing," I answered. "In addition to our children and parents, we all have some responsibility to and for the rest of our family. The nature and extent of this responsibility obviously depends on

---

> Focus, balance, power,
> and spin control are the secrets
> to appropriately using
> your resources.

Great! All the Time!

many things, such as closeness of the relationship and geographical proximity, but, generally speaking, your family should be next in your prioritized list of responsibilities."

"And friends?" he asked, winding up his backswing again.

I let loose a long sigh, which stopped Sol's serve. "What is a true friend, after all?"

He stood up and looked at me. "What do you mean?"

"Well, while most of us may think we have lots of friends, most of those we believe are true friends are in reality mere acquaintances, who are part of our larger community. True friends are those whom you can call upon for almost anything within reason and know you will be able to get it from them. Conversely, a true friend is one to whom you would give anything you owned, if you saw he truly needed it more than you did."

"Okay," he said, with a shrug of his shoulders. "So now that you answered your own question, let's move on. What about your community?"

"That's even more amorphous than figuring out what a true friend is."

"Give it whirl anyway," Sol egged me on, as he popped a light serve right in front of me.

"Well," I started, as I lobbed the volley back to the front wall and we hit the ball back and forth. "Except for a person who lives as a true hermit, all of us have a need to live as part of a community.

The Third Lesson

The right to live in a community carries with it the responsibility to do our part to care for that community."

"Which means?" Sol asked.

"Which means that some of us recognize and fulfill that responsibility more than others. Ideally, the needs and desires of the community do not significantly adversely affect our individual needs and desires. Balancing our individual and communal needs and desires determines the relative priority of our responsibility to the community at any given time. We invest our resources in our community; unfortunately, we often only contribute our property in the form of taxes and elect communal leaders to spend those taxes most effectively. Those of us who are more community-minded also contribute our resources of self, time, effort, energy, emotion, intellect, property, and people to otherwise serve the common good."

Sol didn't comment on what I had said, as he picked up the speed and power of his returns to take up the silence. Finally, I saw a good chance at a kill shot and took it.

"Yes!" I exclaimed. "Nothing but power!" I gloated, as I grabbed up the ball and stepped into the service box.

"So, speaking of power," Sol said, as he stepped back into the back court. "What about business? How do you see it fitting in?"

"Well, as we discussed last week, and it

Great! All the Time!

made lots of sense, contrary to the commonly held view that the customer in business is always right and of prime importance, in reality the relative responsibilities to investors, employers, employees, and customers should follow that order."

I sent a hard serve to Sol's backhand corner. He turned towards the ball and slapped it against the back wall. "Why?" he asked, as the ball left his racquet and arched back toward the bottom of the front wall again.

I dove toward the front, but did not make it far enough to catch the ball. Acting casual, I just rolled up onto one elbow and looked at Sol and answered. "Because, as we said, without investors, there would be no employers; without whom there would be no employees; and, without whom there would be no goods and services for customers to come and purchase. While employees, employers, and investors have the responsibility to be truthful and honest in their behavior towards those lower than themselves in this order, their primary responsibility is to those above them."

Sol picked the ball up and looked at me, still sprawled on the floor. "So that about does it then, doesn't it? You look like you've had enough for today."

"Does what?" I asked as I pulled myself back up. "You still haven't told me how to figure out what resources to use in what amounts to do the right thing."

The Third Lesson

"Well, I can't tell you that," he said, as he turned toward the door of the court. "It depends too much on the facts and circumstances at the time you have to make a decision."

"So you can't tell me anything to help me?" I asked, as I got up and followed him out.

"I'll tell you two things, really quickly." He winked and smiled at me. "But then, I have to go talk to a nice young lady about her great-grandchildren."

"Okay," I said. "Shoot."

Sol sat down on the bleachers and began putting his racquet and balls in his bag. "Regardless of their relative positions in the hierarchy, those to whom and for whom our values make us responsible have and will continue to have needs and desires, most of which we are going to have to fulfill. If everyone to whom and for whom our values make us responsible will buy into the concept that we will only use those things in life we truly need and not waste resources, then life will be much more satisfying for all of us."

"But you still haven't answered the question of how I figure out how much of what resources are needed to do the right thing."

Sol reached into his bag, pulled out a ball, sat it down on the bench right next to me, and gave it a faultless twist, which left it spinning perfectly, without moving side to side. "I already told you," the old man said, with a wicked grin. "Focus,

Great! All the Time!

balance, power, spin control, and practice, practice, practice."

I was hypnotized by the spinning ball and didn't notice that Sol was leaving until he was just disappearing around the corner.

"Go home and think about that for a week," he bellowed. "Then write me another letter."

Despite the hour we had just spent together, supposedly discussing it, I wanted to yell to Sol as he slipped away, "But, I still don't understand how to get it all done."

The Third Lesson

> Focus, balance, power, spin control, and practice, practice, practice.

The Fourth Letter

I continued to feel like a lost ball in tall weeds all week long. Nonetheless, another letter Sol had demanded and another letter I had to write.

Dear Sol,
I think I understand all of the relationship and resources stuff we discussed the other day. Nonetheless, I am still having problems deciding how much of which resources to use for which responsibilities I have to fulfill.
I need for you to help me come up with some method to make things work better for me in all of my relationships.

The Fourth Lesson

As I arrived, my old friend was sitting on the bleachers, looking less lively than usual. "What's wrong, Sol?" I asked, as I sat down beside him.

"Nothing," he mumbled. "I'm Great! All the time!" he said, though with much less enthusiasm than I had ever seen.

"You seem pretty tired."

"I am tired," he said, starting to perk up a bit. "But that doesn't mean that I can't still be Great! All the time!"

I didn't hurry him to play. Instead, I took out my letter and gave it to him to read. "Read over this while we wait to get started."

Sol took the letter and began to review it. I felt good as he seemed to be nodding in agreement.

"So you've got the types of resources idea down pretty well and you seem to be on your way to solving your problems with the balance stuff, huh?" he asked.

Great! All the Time!

"Yeah. But there still doesn't seem to be enough time in the day to get done with everything I think I need to get done."

"Yes, but you're well on your way because you've recognized the need for something I call the P9 Principle."

"What the heck is the P9 Principle?" I asked.

"If you are going to get through life as easily as possible, then you have to master the art of cycling your resources."

"Cycling my resources?"

"Yes," he explained. "All of us start out life with the same amount of self, time, effort, energy, emotion, intellect, property, and people. In order to get through life, you have to keep creating, using, and recreating all of those resources, all the time. That is what's called 'cycling your resources.'"

"Well, great!" I whined. "Another thing to have to worry about." I went on complaining. "First, I have to worry about all of my different relationships; then, I have to worry about who is the

> All of us start out life with the same amount of self, time, effort, energy, emotion, intellect, property, and people.

The Fourth Lesson

highest and most of those to whom and for whom I am responsible; and, now, you want me to worry about cycling my resources too!" I started to get a little bit too excited. "This is getting to be just a little bit much."

"Relaaaaaaaaax," he said, putting his hand on my shoulder. "Remember a few weeks ago when we first started to talk about this?"

"Yes."

"Remember how you said you wanted to learn for yourself how to be 'Great! All the time!'?"

"Yes."

"Recall, even though I told you it wouldn't be easy, how you said you'd be willing to try because you've never been afraid of hard work?"

"Yes."

"Have you forgotten, we agreed in the beginning that this was not going to be a 'quick-fix' kind of thing?"

"No. So?"

"So this is some of the 'hard work' part." He

Cycling your resources

In order to get through life,
you have to keep creating, using,
and recreating all of your resources,
all the time.

Great! All the Time!

smiled because he knew he had me.

"Fine, then!" I mocked some more anger for good measure. "So how do I master this resource cycling thing and how is it going to answer my questions about handling competing relationships?

Well, first of all, none of your relationships compete with each other because they all really complement one another. Second, you tie cycling your resources together with doing the right thing by using the P9 Principle."

"So, again," I asked. "What on earth is the P9 Principle?"

"The P9 Principle stands for the idea that proper perception, planning, preparation, and practice promote practically perfect performance."

"What does that mean?"

"Just what it says. You see, most people just bumble through life without really perceiving what they want to get from of it; and, without planning, preparing, and practicing to succeed in it. So, they just waste the majority of their resources, chasing whatever it is the last person they listened to told them they needed to have or do or be. They don't understand what a good life really is and, therefore, they don't plan to live well. If they do plan, then they don't prepare and then practice what they plan. So, most of them just get lost in the pit of poor performance, instead of promoting the practically perfect performance of being Great! All the time!"

"What exactly do you mean?"

The Fourth Lesson

"Well," Sol leaned back to rest a little. "Let's take a look at your average day, prior to last month. On your normal day before we started learning together, what did you do all day?"

"I got up at six and went to the gym; then, I went to work until about seven at night; then I came home, ate a bite alone, and watched television until midnight, when I went to sleep."

"Why?"

"I don't know. Because that's the way that I've always done it, I guess."

"Why?" Sol demanded again.

"I don't know. Like I said, it's just the way I've always done it, I guess."

"Okay," he said. "Did you think about any of your relationships as you were doing what you did all day?"

"No, not really."

"So you just kind of lived down in a pit all by your poor little self then, didn't you?"

"I guess so." That realization hurt a little bit.

The P9 Principle

Proper perception, planning, preparation, and practice promote practically perfect performance.

Great! All the Time!

"But, at least now, I'm trying to do something about it."

"So," Sol asked, "over the past few weeks, did you start thinking more about your relationships?"

"Yes."

"And what did you do about them?"

"I started thinking, planning, and doing more things about them?"

"Like what?" Sol asked.

"Like getting up earlier and going to the office later so that I could get in a workout and still make it to morning prayers before work. Then, I started planning meetings earlier in the day, so everyone could leave on time. Plus, I started making appointments to do things with my wife and kids and volunteer for things, like stuffing boxes at the food bank."

"And did you feel more like you were climbing out of your pit than you were before?"

I thought about it for a second. "Yes."

"And did you have to do some planning, preparation, and practicing to get all of that done last week?"

"Yes."

"And, did you feel like you were living better, when you were doing more of that 'stuff' last week?"

"Yes."

"And, was life more peaceful for you?"

"Yes."

The Fourth Lesson

"And, was it more satisfying?"

"Yes."

"And, did it seem like it was practically perfect?"

"Yes."

"Well then," Sol said as he patted me on the back. "You've just learned for yourself that the P9 Principle works, haven't you? You've learned for yourself that 'Proper perception, planning, preparation, and practice promote practically perfect performance,' haven't you?"

A light bulb went off. "Ah-hah!"

"Ah-haaaaaah!" Sol mocked at me. "And, if you would be using the P9 Principle all the time, then, you would be perceiving, planning, preparing, and practicing to do the right thing all the time, which would be more peaceful and satisfying, wouldn't it?"

"Yes."

"Then you have just learned for yourself, the meaning of 'Greatness!'"

"Which is?"

"Which is the peaceful …" He touched his thumbs to his middle fingers, as if he was entering into a meditative chant. "And satisfied …" He then opened his hands as if to catch a ball in his palms. "State of mind …" He closed his eyes and tilted his head back for a second and then reopened them and continued, "Resulting from the use of proper perception, planning, preparation, and practice …"

Great! All the Time!

He counted to four with his right fingers. "To transform your values, vision, and mission ..." He counted to three with his left. "Into performance of the balanced creation ..." He held both hands like he was cradling a huge ball. "Highest and best use, ..." He clasped his hands together. "And recreation ..." He cradled the ball again. "Of life's precious resources of self, time, effort, energy, emotion, intellect, property and people ..." He counted them off on the fingers of his right and then left hands. "To do the right thing, which is the best thing in the present circumstances ..." He pointed his index finger forward. "For the optimal balance of the highest ..." He seemed to measure his own height. "And the most ..." He lowered his hand and turned it palm up again. "Of those to whom ..." He pointed his finger up. "And for whom ..." He flowed his fingers over the waters again. "Our values make us responsible."

I tried to follow everything that he was saying and doing in order to bring it into some order. "That's an awfully long definition of Greatness!" I said.

"Do you want me to go over it again?"

"Yes, please."

He started his hand dance again, but I interrupted him. "Can we try this one time without all the hand signals?" I asked. "Because they are confusing me."

Sol smiled, closed his eyes, and shook his head a little. "I guess you think the hand signals are

The Fourth Lesson

a little hokey, huh?"

"Yeah. I don't know." I was a little embarrassed for some reason and I blushed a little for trying to argue with the master. "Yeah, I guess it seems a little hokey, but mostly it's just distracting me."

"I know how you feel," he said, putting his hand on my shoulder, which was comforting and made me feel more connected to him. "Because I used to feel the same way." He wrapped his arm around my shoulder. "But then I found out something." He leaned closer to me. "Let me tell you what I found out."

"What?" I asked quietly.

Sol paused a second and then started to whisper, "Hoke is good."

"What?"

"Hoke is it!" Sol started to smile a little. And, then, with a big grin he said, "'Hoke' is the real thing!"

I started to laugh as I thought to myself. Great! I've got a whacked-out senior citizen mentor with a weird sense of humor who is stuck in the seventies chanting parodies of Coke commercials at me. This is just peachy!

"Great!" I said.

"No, honestly. The hand signals really help if you use them correctly," He asked, "Do you know how a martial artist uses katas to practice his art?"

"Yes."

Great! All the Time!

"Well, people who are Great! All the time! are martial artists of another kind."

"What do you mean?"

"Well, they're not just martial artists, they're 'marshal' artists; and what they marshal is their resources."

"Okay …." I hesitated, as I felt a little unsure at that point.

"They marshal their resources of self, time, effort, energy, emotion, intellect, property, and people to do the right thing at the present time in the present circumstances."

"Okay …," I said tentatively.

Sol put his hand on my shoulder. "But for those of you who are mentally impaired and can't dance because you can't follow both words and movements at the same time, we will do a remedial review." He smiled warmly at me.

"Thank you."

"Here we go." He paused and looked at me. "Are you sure you're ready?"

"Absolutely."

"Okay, pay attention," he said, putting his hands behind his back.

"Greatness! -- is the peaceful and satisfied state of mind resulting from the use of proper perception, planning, preparation, and practice to transform your values, vision, and mission into performance of the balanced creation, highest and best use, and recreation of life's precious resources

The Fourth Lesson

of self, time, effort, energy, emotion, intellect, property, and people to do the right thing, which is the best thing in the present circumstances for the optimal balance of the highest priority and the most of those to whom and for whom our values make us responsible."

I thought about what he was saying for a second to let it sink in.

Sol released his hands from behind his back and picked up his racquet and said, "Come on," as he got up from the bleachers. "Let's go play a game and I'll show you what it all means."

We walked to the center of the court and he turned and looked at me. "Okay, kid. Here's where you get your first and last lesson in how to play racquetball Great! All the time!"

"Great!" I had been eagerly waiting for this.

"Do everything that I show you how to do today and you will always play racquetball and the rest of life Great! All the time!"

"Great!" I was more than eagerly waiting for this.

"Do everything that I show you today and you'll be able to beat me just like that kid you saw a few weeks ago."

"Great! Already!" I was dying to get on with this. "Can we just get on with the lesson?"

"Okay," he chuckled, knowing he was vexing me. "The first thing you have to do," he said, as he bent over straight-legged and palmed the floor.

Great! All the Time!

"Is to know that 'you' are your most precious resource." He stood back up straight and began to stretch up high on both of his tiptoes. "And in order to marshal yourself as your most precious resource, you sometimes have to stretch yourself farther than you have ever stretched before."

I just stood there watching the old man do calisthenics. He came back down and pointed his hand at me. "Well?"

"Well, what?"

"Well, let's see how far you can stretch."

"Well," I started to bend over at the waist and let my hands hang down, the tips of my fingers hardly even touching my ankles much less going as far has his did. "I know I can't palm the floor like you."

"Not yet," he said, pressing down on the middle of my back with one hand while his other hand palmed the floor again. "But stretch just a little farther each day than you did the day before and everything in your life will get a little easier."

We came back up and started to reach over our heads. "First, on both toes," he said, taking an even stance. Then he shifted over to his right foot, dropped his right hand down, balanced with his left arm even higher in the air, and stood like a ballerina. "Then, on one toe."

I followed suit, but only on the ball of my right foot.

He held the perfectly balanced stretch for

The Fourth Lesson

a second and then switched feet and arms. "And, then, on the other toe."

Sol came back down and then lunged out with his hands and right foot going forward in what was almost a front split.

I followed him about half the way down.

He stretched his right hand, arm, and shoulder a little further than the left. "First one way," he said changing arms. "And then the other."

I went as far as I could, which wasn't far, but farther than I had before.

Sol then pivoted his feet and turned the other direction to repeat the stretch with the other leg and both arms.

We finished stretching and Sol gave me the ball for the favor of the first serve. I bounced it a few times and thought about where I wanted to put the serve. I decided on a quick stab to his low backhand and slapped the ball hard.

I must have telegraphed the move, however, because I heard Sol whack the ball solidly back

---

> Stretch just a little farther each day
> than you did the day before
> and everything in your life
> will get a little easier.

Great! All the Time!

down the backhand wall for a rollout.

He grabbed the ball quickly as it came back to him and began walking toward me in the service box. "You wasted too much time thinking about the serve." We traded positions. "As soon as the other guy is ready—"

"I know," I said. "'Get to it, now!' applies as much to serves as it does to returns, right?"

Sol smiled as he looked at me and I nodded that I was ready to receive the serve. He quickly dropped the ball and smacked it before it hit the ground for a perfect ace to the same spot where I had just sent it. It went by so fast that I didn't even have time to move.

"Just take the shot," he said as he let the ball fly. "Don't wait and don't think, because you have already perceived, planned, prepared, and practiced this performance a thousand times before."

He sneakily slipped a second ball out of his pocket and quickly served again without even looking at it. "You've planned." Splat! It was another ace.

He took a third ball out and served it the same way to the same spot still not even appearing to look at the ball as it fell from his hand. "You've prepared." Splat! Another ace.

He slipped a fourth ball out of his second pocket and served it in quick succession. "You've practiced." Splat. Another ace.

He slipped a fifth ball out of his second

The Fourth Lesson

pocket. "And you've practiced, again." Splat! And another ace.

Sol stood up and looked at me standing there flat-footed and dumbfounded. He walked past me and picked up all five balls, which were now pretty much lying together in the same corner. "So, just perceive the need, and then, plan, prepare, and practice to promote practically perfect performance to do the right thing, right here and now, and move on."

Sol walked back past me, in the middle of the backcourt, as he put four of the balls back into his pockets. "Got it?" he asked.

"Yeah."

"Good," Sol said, as he moved for the service box. "Five-zip for the old guy." He must have somehow heard what I was thinking.

"But I wasn't ready for the last four!" I protested. "I didn't even know that you had that many balls in your shorts." I grinned at the double entendre.

"Oh," he said. "I'm sorry." He tossed the last ball to me and came back to the backcourt. "My bad. You go ahead and serve." He motioned me to the box. "But, it's still zip serving five."

As soon as I was in the box, without even looking to see if Sol was ready, I whacked a forehand serve, which skimmed down the side wall. It must have worked, I thought, because it didn't come back. I looked back and saw Sol lunged out with

Great! All the Time!

his racquet just a few inches short of the wall and a smile on his face.

"I don't have any extra balls to trick you with," I said, as I motioned for the ball in the back of the room.

Sol made a show about bringing it back to me. Then he caught my next serve solidly on his backhand side and killed it to get back in box.

Sol put one past me hugging the forehand wall. When it didn't come back to him, he looked back and saw me, imitating him, by stretching a lunge, just a few inches farther than I had done just before, as I let the ball get by me.

"Stretching just a little farther each time?" he asked, with approval.

"At least I'm trainable," I replied, as I stood back up.

"We'll see," he said, as he snapped off the next serve.

We played a few more rounds with me scoring some and him scoring some, until we got down to a game point.

"Ten serving nine for the win." I said.

The volley lasted longer than any we'd ever had. Finally, Sol just barely got his racquet on one of my shots and left me the perfect opportunity for a rollout kill shot to win the game. While I had won many games before, nothing gave me quite the same satisfaction as finally putting this one away.

We met in the court and I asked, "Did I really

The Fourth Lesson

win that game or did you let me win that game?"

"Well, Greatness! sometimes comes through letting others enjoy a modicum of success," Sol smugly said under his breath.

"That doesn't really answer my question."

"And the most effective leader always lets all of those around him think they are in control." He smiled a knowing smile.

I thought for a second. "But you still haven't answered my question."

"Do you think you won that game?"

I thought for a second more. "Yes."

"Good," he said. "Then if you're happy with that thought, I'm ecstatic." He let his racquet hang from his wrist strap. "Well, my job is done here today." He patted me on the back with his left hand and shook my hand with his right. "I've got to go now. This week, go home and write me a letter about how you are going to use the P9 Principle to cycle your resources to do the right thing all the time."

"Yes, sir," I said, saluting smartly with my left

> Greatness! sometimes comes through letting others enjoy a modicum of success.

Great! All the Time!

hand, half in jest and half in formality for a moment, like I was saying goodbye to a senior master.

Sol let go of my hand and started down the hall. He yelled over his shoulder at me, "I'll try to see you next week. We'll tie everything together for you and, hopefully, we'll learn the real meaning of life." Then he stopped and turned around and pointed back at me. "But if I don't make it back on time, then you go out there, this week and every week, and be Great! All the time!" He smiled fully, but weakly; and then, he turned and walked away.

I pointed back at him to make a long distance connection. "You, too, Sol." I said softly, with a tightness rising in my throat. As I started to well up and cry just a little, I whispered, "You, too."

The Fourth Lesson

> Go out there,
> this week and every week,
> and be
> Great! All the time!

The Fifth Letter

Remembering to "Get To It, Now!" I went home after the game and thought about what we had just discussed that morning. I doodled and scratched on a pad of paper as I pondered the meaning of it all.

Several hours later, I had finished my capstone letter to Sol.

Dear Sol,
You asked me "how am I going to use the P9 Principle to cycle my resources to do the right thing all the time?"
I have been working with the things we have learned together over the last month in order to live a more peaceful and satisfying life and this is what I've come up with.
Which of my relationships gets what types and amounts of my resources of self, time, effort, energy, emotion, intellect, property, and people

Great! All the Time!

depends on the facts and circumstances involved at the time that things are happening. I do know, however, that I am going to have to, first, perceive the need, and then, plan, prepare, and practice in advance what to do and how to do it.

First, I am going to have to realize what my values are, which values really derive from my relationships themselves. Then I am going to have to visualize a vision that shows me living my life in accordance with those values. Only, after I have that vision firmly in mind, can I define my mission to take concrete steps to obtain it.

This means that I am going to have to determine what objectives I need to achieve in order to do what is best for each and all of those with whom I have a relationship. Working from the top of the hierarchy down, I am going to have to perceive the needs, and then, plan, prepare, and practice nurturing each and all of my relationships. If something concerning a relationship lower on my hierarchy conflicts with the values, vision, and mission of a higher relationship, then either I will have to resolve the conflict or the lower relationship will have to yield.

The best way to plan the use of my resources for the various tasks in front of me is to plot them out on a calendar and constantly be looking forward to what is coming up in the next hour, day, week, month, and year. Keeping a list of all of the objectives for all of the relationships with that calendar will help

The Fifth Letter

me stay focused on what is truly important in my life as opposed to letting unimportant things creep into my schedule.

Sometimes, I have discovered, the emergent needs of a lower relationship may develop a greater need for resources that were originally planned for a higher relationship. For example, I recently planned on doing cardiovascular exercise for an hour at the gym to recreate my self. I had just gotten started when my son came up and told me that he had forgotten several key steps of his new weightlifting routine. At that moment, in those circumstances, he needed that same time, for me to help him, more than I needed it to recreate myself. I instinctively thought, at the moment he asked for help, "What is the highest and best use of my resources of self, time, effort, energy, emotion, intellect, property and people at this moment?" Obviously, the highest and best use was helping to train my son for a better life and do my own cardiovascular workout by running in place as I helped him.

Second, I am going to have to look at what types and amounts of the various resources I have available, and then, plan how to either use those resources that I have or prepare to and create or recreate enough of the right type of resources needed to get as many as possible of the jobs requested done. Resource cycling is a constant process.

Time being the most limited resource for most people, I have learned that we all have to

Great! All the Time!

maximize our use of it. Often this is done by doing two things at once, such as reading while working out on a treadmill. Another way to create more time is to simplify life and eliminate tasks. (Do any of us really need to watch soap operas during the day or Letterman at night?) We can also shift tasks to others who should and could help us through life. (Kids are supposed to help parents with yard work, despite the fact, they will tell you, that no one else's father makes their friends do it.)

Third, I am going to have to convince others concerned in each of my relationships that they, too, will have to invest their own share of their own resources, perceive their needs, and plan, prepare, practice, and perform for themselves to do the right thing.

Fourth, I am going to have to say "No" at some time to some of those to whom and for whom my values make me responsible. At some point, they and I are just not going to have or be able to create or recreate enough resources to do what is being asked. At that point, I am going to have to say "No," and whoever is making the request is going to have to change their needs, in order to get by, within the resources that we have available. Someone has to be the leader in any relationship. Leadership in a relationship is all about knowing when you have to say "No" and being able to do so, whenever you have to, but only when you have to.

Fifth, I am going to have to "Get To It, Now!"

The Fifth Letter

I will have to constantly stay in touch with every person, place, thing, or idea, with which I have a relationship, in order to perceive each relationship's needs. And, once I have perceived a need, I will have to immediately plan, prepare, and practice to promote the practically perfect performance of fulfilling that need. I will have to live in the present, do all of today's work today, and finish each day's step in my long-term plans each day.

And, so, Sol, that is how I think I can use the P9 Principle to do the right thing all the time.

Sharing the Message

I showed up the next week ready to share my message with Sol and found his racquet sitting on the bleachers where he normally did. On the racquet was an envelope containing the following note:

I am sorry that I am not able to be here in person to tie everything together with you. You, however, obviously have learned for yourself how to be Great! All the time!

I promised you I would tell you the real meaning of life. It is best explained using some excerpts from something else that was written a long time ago. It goes something like this:

It is suitable to eat and drink and enjoy pleasure with all one's labor that he toils beneath the sun during the brief span of his life that God has given him, for that is his lot. Furthermore, every

Great! All the Time!

man to whom God has given riches and possessions and has given him the power to enjoy them, possess his share, and be happy in his work: this is the gift of God. For he shall remember that the days of his life are not many, while God provides him with the joy of his heart.

Go, eat your bread with joy and drink your wine with a glad heart, for God has already approved your deeds. Let your garments always be white, and your head never lack oil.

Enjoy life with the wife you love through all fleeting days of your life that He has granted you beneath the sun, all of your futile existence, for that is your compensation in life and in your toil, which you exert beneath the sun. Whatever you are able to do with your might, do it. For there is neither doing nor reckoning nor knowledge nor wisdom in the grave where you are going.

The sum of the matter, when all has been considered, is to fear God and keep His commandments, for that is man's duty. For God will judge every deed – even everything hidden – whether good or evil.

Great! All the Time!

The sum of the matter, when all has been considered: fear God and keep His commandments, for that is man's whole duty.

Use this racquet to share this message with whoever may come your way and need it. Now, go out there and be

Great! All the time!

Solomon T. Wise

Epilogue

As I sat there crying, a man about my age came up and asked "Are you okay?"

"Yes," I replied, as I sat up and cleared my throat. "I may be sad, but I'm still Great! All the time!"

"I saw you beat Sol, the King, last week," he said. "I've never played this game before, could you show me how?"

"Sure," I said, handing him Sol's old racquet. "I can help you learn to play this game, and to live the rest of your life to be Great! All the time! But only if we can 'Get to it, now!'"

In Memory Of

PAUL SIMOES D'ENCARNACAO, Ph.D.
1929 – 1998
A good racquetball player, a better psychologist, and a best friend who truly was

Great! All the time!

Greatness!

Greatness! -- is the peaceful and satisfied state of mind resulting from the use of proper perception, planning, preparation, and practice to transform your values, vision, and mission into performance of the balanced creation, highest and best use, and recreation of life's precious resources of self, time, effort, energy, emotion, intellect, property, and people to do the right thing, which is the best thing in the present circumstances for the optimal balance of the highest priority and the most of those to whom and for whom our values make us responsible.

The Search for "Greatness!"

"Greatness!" resides in all of us, if only we are willing to perceive it and achieve it. Too many times, however, "Greatness!" goes unrecognized. At RTMC, we are constantly "Reaching to motivate change" and the person we want to reach immediately is you.

If you know of anyone who is practically perfectly marshalling their life's resources to do the best thing for the highest priority and most of those to whom and for whom their values make them responsible, then please register at our web site, www.RTMC.org, and leave us a message about them. If we like their story, we will send them and you a nice red "Great! All the time!" button and enter them into consideration for the American "Greatness!" Awards to give them the recognition they deserve.

The American "Greatness!" Awards are funded by the proceeds of this and other button books published by RTMC. Watch for our coming titles. Register at www.RTMC.org for more offers and information.

Whatever you do, go out there and be

Great! All the time!